Astrology

Character, Essence, and the Nature of the 12 Zodiac Signs

Valerie W. Holt

Contents

Introduction

Some people might associate it with some type of dark art. You might not know much about it because it was banned from religion long ago. Others consider it to be a joke or at least not to be taken seriously. It's also looked upon as an old form of entertainment that has managed to withstand the test of time.

For others, it is a part of their daily routine, their last stop in the paper or their favorite application on their phone. These folks think it's a fun thing to do but might not take it that seriously.

On the other hand, there are seekers, who do take *it* seriously and know it to be a valuable tool that helps them learn more about themselves, others, and the world around them. They know it can be a way for them to find healthier relationships and find meaning in their lives.

If you haven't figured it out already, we are talking about astrology, an ancient language involving celestial bodies. Astrology acknowledges that factors like our surroundings and our genes influence who we are, but it also takes into consideration the state of the solar system at the time of our birth.

This book will explain the zodiac signs and what they mean regarding character and the influence they can have on us. It will start with the history and basics of astrology before going into the more detailed descriptions. This will give you a better understanding of the world you live in and the people around you.

Chapter 1
The Origins of Astrology

Astrology dates back to the Babylonian civilization, who created the first astrological charts and used them to monitor the seasons and other celestial events. When they looked at the heavens, they did not distinguish between astronomy and astrology and they were treated as if they were the same science. It was impressive and innovative for them, especially given the time and the limited resources they had available to them to achieve as much as they did. They thought that only five planets existed: Mars, Saturn, Mercury, Venus, and Jupiter. When creating their detailed charts, they also included the sun, the moon, and stars.

The Babylonians tracked 12 constellations that they named after different animals. They used the passage of these and the placement of the sun and planets to measure celestial time if separated into identifiable and equal segments. They even gave the planets their own unique powers, for instance, Mars was red, and they thought it was related to anger and even war. Of course, today we would not consider this to be an exact science, but it was how the Babylonians were able to have a better understanding of their world and even the other planets.

The Greeks, 2000 years later, made significant progress in both astrology and astronomy after studying Plato and Aristotle. They approached astronomy and astrology in a more analytical way. It was the Greeks who created the zodiac, or the circle of animals, giving more validity to what the Babylonians had done. It took decades of tracking the stars and moon for early astrologers to figure out that it took twelve months, or lunar cycles, for the sun to come back to its original position after orbiting around the planets.

The Greeks continued to study the heavens and made many advances; they figured out that the Earth was round, not flat, that it circled the sun, and they even made a precise technique to determine an eclipse. Many Greek astrology texts and charts survived and had become known as the foundation for what we know as astrology today.

Their contributions of the zodiac and figuring out how to determine the placement of the planets led to horoscopes. Every person has a horoscope that is based on the placements of the sun, moon, planets, and stars at a specific moment in time, most often that of a person's birth. Talented astrologers use this information to create a detailed chart that contains information about a person's personality traits, compatible signs, future challenges, and even likely future events. Skilled astrologers can even include information such as a person's mood during specific months

4

which they base on what planet is in which house at that particular time. If conducted properly, astrology can be an enlightening and insightful science.

There are many ways to find horoscopes, such as the newspaper, the internet, and phone applications. However, these are vague and are not tailored to a specific individual. If you want a detailed chart dedicated specifically for you, the best thing for you to do is go a trained and authentic astrologer. The amount of information you will receive in an astrology profile is unbeatable.

Astrology's popularity has not remained steady, throughout the centuries it has fallen in and out of popularity. Astrology is more popular now than it has been in a long time. People all around the world are learning and exploring astrology, which keeps it alive and well. This also suggests that if there were absolutely no validity to the science, then it would have vanished long ago.

Chapter 2
The Fundamentals of Astrology

If you go outside and look at the night sky, you will see that the moon, planets, and stars appear to orbit around us. This would suggest that Earth is the center of the universe, and from our view, that is exactly what it looks like, even if we do know different. However, this is how astrologers study the universe, with a geocentric view, since they are observing and studying the interaction between Earth and the rest of the universe. As these celestial bodies orbit the earth, they are traveling through the 12 zodiac signs. When you check your daily horoscope, it is about the position of the sun, but there are four factors that go into astrology: the planets, the signs, the houses, and the aspects.

Astrology acknowledges the existence of nine planets, which includes Pluto. Some people will argue that Pluto is not a planet, and scientists have gone back and forth about this, but in Astrology there is no debate. Nine planets are included regardless of how the debates go, as this has been the way for centuries. In astrology, everything has a meaning and everything is important, you will see how everything begins to fit together like a puzzle to create a complete and thorough astrological profile.

Sun: The sun tells an astrologer about the inner person, what is at an individual's core. It can also reveal information about a person's main concerns or worries and describes the general tone of one's being and changes every month.

Moon: A person's emotions and feelings are represented by the moon, including their imagination and how receptive they are to the world around them, which of course can influence mood. The moon influences timing and rhythm, thus affecting our ability to adapt to change. The moon changes sign every two or three days, while also going through its different lunar phases.

Mercury: Common sense and reason are represented by this planet, such as order and the spoken or written word. The learning process and the acquiring of skills are also associated with this planet. Mercury also represents evaluation and all that is rational and changes signs every three to four weeks.

Venus: Just like the name of the famous Goddess, this planet is linked to pleasure and beauty. In addition to aesthetics, this also includes sociability, harmony, attraction, and eroticism. Venus changes signs every four to five weeks.

Mars: This planet signifies a person's drive, courage, determination, spontaneity, and energy.

Mars also represents the manner at which a person goes about achieving a goal even if that includes simple aggression. Mars changes signs every six to seven weeks.

Jupiter: Jupiter embodies hope, faith, luck, spirituality, justice, and purpose. Jupiter also represents spiritual growth and wisdom, and it changes signs every twelve to thirteen months.

Saturn: This planet represents our limitations and boundaries. It explains the way a person experiences "reality," and the places they meet resistance in their lives. Saturn is also associated with laws, rules, morals, and our conscience, and whether we choose to abide by laws or rules. Saturn is also connected to our concentration and our powers of endurance, including reserve and caution. Saturn only crosses through a sign every two or three years.

Uranus: This planet rules originality, inspiration, insightfulness, and intuition. Uranus represents a person's receptiveness to the unknown, unusual, and new. On the other end of the spectrum, this planet also represents a wrong-headed uncooperativeness or unacceptance; this can often be associated with astrology itself. Uranus changes signs every seven years.

Neptune: Neptune is associated with mystical experiences and pseudo-realities, such as illusion, deception, and dishonest appearances. It is because of this that it can be difficult to differentiate when perception changes to deception, for instance, dreams or day dreams. Neptune also represents healing and changes signs every ten to twelve years.

Pluto: This tiny planet represents how people cope with power, both their own and other people's. Pluto is associated with transformation and rebirth, which also includes the cycle of death and regeneration. Pluto's orbit causes it to change signs every twelve to fifteen years. However, this can vary.

Imagine the sun as a sphere in the middle and the orbit as a circle around the sun, the closer the planet is to the sun, the smaller the circle, therefore the shorter the orbit. Since each of the planets, sun, and moon each hold their own meanings, it is easy to see how their specific placement can have an impact on your life. Of course, this depends on what house and sign they are in at a specific time, and because it can change, so too can the influence they have over you. A great example of this is how you feel from either a waning or waxing sun.

An example of this would be, Pisces who are particularly sensitive to the moon, which can greatly influence their mood. They have a tendency to be more emotional during a full moon, but at the same time, it can also serve as a form of inspiration for them too. So even though it can be emotional, it can also be a time for creative growth and development.

Houses

The houses are arranged on a wheel, and the planets can reside in them as well. This is not to be confused with the Zodiac chart, the wheel of houses and the Zodiac wheel are separate. The zodiac chart is associated with the sun's year-long rotation in reference to Earth, or along the ecliptic. The wheel of houses concerns the Earth's 24-hour rotation on its own axis. However, the two wheels do a crossover at certain points which can be found using calculations based on your exact time of birth, and the astronomical coordinates at that exact time. The houses are numbered but do not have names like the zodiac.

This means that planets can be described in two ways, by first having a zodiac sign, as well as being in a house. Imagine them both as gears; they can turn separately, but also together, and when they do, their rotation causes different overlaps. For instance, two people might both be Libras, but one might have the Libra sun in her 12th house, while the other might have it in his first. This would mean that although they are of the same sign, they are completely different types of people. This is one of the reasons why a daily horoscope can be so vague since it only includes the placement of the sun and it assumes everyone is of the same house, which is not true.

The 12 houses are symbols of all the areas that make up human life, and the planets and signs will manifest most powerfully in the part of life that is represented by the house that they fit into on your chart. However, the planets and elements are energies, and the houses are not, they are where the energies are most probable to manifest. The houses are not the experience themselves, but rather fields of experience.

The order of the houses is set to the developmental route of a person's life, and each one has its own set of meanings. The most important houses are the first, fourth, seventh, and tenth, known as the angular houses. They are called this because their cusps overlap with the four special angles, ascendant, I.C., descendant, and M.C., the planets in any of the angular houses will have the most influence and the most impact on you.

First House: This is known as the house of self, it includes self-awareness such as the body, personality, views on life, appearance, self-image, and beginnings. This house determines how we approach things in our lives and how impulsive we are. Any of the planets in this house will have a lot of influence on not only your own personality, but also the ways in which others see you.

Second House: This house represents what you own, whether it be money or possessions, anything that you value. However, this can also include your sense of value or self-worth and self-esteem. These possessions can be everything except for your home since that is included in a different house, so, your car, investments, even your furniture is included in this house. Not only is it physical possessions, but also how you earn and spend money, how you feel about wealth, and your potential for getting it.

Third House: This house is associated with communication and by association with your current environments, such as your family, neighbors, transportation, and any short journeys you might be traveling at the time. This house is also connected to the lower mind which refers to thought patterns, intellect, and early education. In terms of this house, communication denotes everything from gossip, phone calls, text messages, visits, writing, speaking, and reading.

Fourth House: This is the house that contains the home and everything that is connected to it, including both your early, childhood home and your current one. This house is complex because not only is it referring to the actual home, but it also includes, land, family, and personal foundations, such as your deep emotional security that stem from your personal roots. Some astrologers believe that this house is also connected to your parents, while some disagree. Regardless of this, though, it is deeply connected to the way in which you were raised and your upbringing.

The fourth house is a base; it is the focal point of your concrete existence, which includes what is underneath the surface of the Earth. It is because of this that this house is thought to rule what happens at the end of your life in addition to the beginning. This can be incredibly important and useful for those who believe in reincarnation since it can be a wonderful source of information about previous lives. Since it affects your base life, this means that this house will influence your relationships with your parents, emotions, and your home life.

Fifth House: This house is connected to creativity, pleasurable pursuits, and children. The best way to sum up this house is that, it represents who you are and how you enjoy being yourself, which as you know can be a lot of things, just think about the list of things that bring you pleasure, some examples are: love, teaching, hobbies, self-expression, showing love, personal interests, and even gambling. Since pleasure is linked with this house, that means that love, romance, and dating are as well. However, marriage is ruled by a different house. The reason for this is that until recently, marriage was not part of what we know as love and romance, marriage was not usually a choice and had very little to do with love. This is not true today, so when thinking about marriage, it is a good idea to combine the two houses, the fifth and the seventh which deal with cooperative relationships.

Sixth House: The sixth house is what rules deals with our work and daily lives. Think about everything that goes into your day; it is probably much more than you realize and this is the house it is connected to; health, sickness, diet, caretaking, volunteering, civil service work, and tedious daily tasks. However, this is not about your career; that is a different house, but rather the small jobs and tasks that make up your day like your personal hygiene. Your quality of work and how hard you try at the jobs you are faced with is also included in this house, like coping with daily crises.

Seventh House: This is the house that rules marriage because it deals with one-on-one relationships, which is what marriage is. However, it is not only marriage that falls into this, business partners, divorce, enemies, and contracts also fall into this category. The main difference between the romantic affairs in the fifth house and the relationships this house refers to is that these are thought to be more permanent.

Once a relationship in the fifth house has progressed into something monogamous and serious, then it is considered to have moved into the seventh house.

Relationships in this house are about sharing, cooperation, and usually have a function or a purpose in the surrounding community or environment, such as a business. This house can reveal information about any of personal relationships ranging from your marriage to your business partner.

Eighth House: This house is related to the second house, but instead of it being your personal assets it is your joint assets. Most people consider the eight house to be a negative house, but this is not true—it is just misunderstood. It seems like the things this house rules are simply not connected, but they are in the sense that they are shared in a relationship and are associated with transformation. These things include taxes, the act of sex, inheritances, legacies, death, wills, regeneration, joint resources, spouse's income, personal sacrifice, losses, alimony, and bankruptcy. Even though these things seem inherently negative, they all represent an opportunity to transform and in the end become more powerful, whether that be through joint income or inheriting money from a loss in the family. Shifting your perception will make this house seem a lot less undesirable.

Ninth House: This is the house that deals with higher education, law, learning, religion, ethics, long journeys, dreams, and spirituality. This is also the house that deals with big ideas and big thoughts like dreams, visions, ceremonies, and rituals. The understanding in this house is a bit more complex than that of the third house because it is linked with your need to discover and understand abstract or generalized ideas, such as finding the meaning of things. This is the higher mind and while the third house deals with the concrete, the ninth deals with the abstract. For example, contact with other cultures and going to a fortune teller would both fall under this house.

Tenth House: This represents status and prestige, such as your reputation both in and out of the workplace. Even if having a lot of money has a lot to do with our status in our culture, this house is not about finances or even gaining it. This house desires success because of honor and social status. That being said, it is only natural that this house also includes recognition, politicians, sense of duty and personal achievements. This house is connected to the most public areas of your life and involves your career, not the daily tasks you have to do. This is another angular house and any planet in this house is incredibly important. The ruling planet in this house will strongly impact your general reputation and your career.

Eleventh House: This is the house that deals with the public as well, but is not associated with your status or reputation. This is the house that represents friends, memberships, social groups, humanitarian interests, self-realization, legislation, and liberty. This house represents your local and chosen communities, the people you choose to surround yourself with and the groups you join.

Twelfth House: This house refers to the subconscious mind, it is our hidden self. This is a complex house, and it rules things such as limitations, frustrations, mental illness, subconscious habit patterns, and in the end our own undoing. There is also a physical aspect to this house as well, and it includes things that tend to keep us from participating fully in our everyday lives. Things like secrets, hidden enemies, and self-sacrifices are all examples of things that stop us from being fully present. It can also stand for things that we have no control over such as kidnapping, bribery, isolation, and even murder.

It is inside these houses that we find our zodiac signs, but before you learn more about each of the signs, you must first have a grasp of the aspects. The aspects are what connect two or more planets. This is the simplest breakdown of what an aspect is, they include things like conjunctions, angularity, squares, oppositions, trines, and sextiles. However, these are things that a knowledgeable astrologer will understand the importance of. For now, you just need to know that aspects play an important role in an astrological reading and the science altogether. They are mathematical and deal with angles and the placement of planets or other celestial bodies in relation to one another.

As you can see, for something that has often not been considered a valid science, a lot goes into a proper astrological reading. For those who only read their daily horoscopes, they are missing out on a wealth of information. It is in your best interest to take as much into account as possible, so you have the most thorough reading. Even if you choose not to go to an astrologer, but are just considering astrology as a fun hobby, the more you know, the better.

Chapter 3
Divisions Within Astrology

The twelve signs are divided equally into masculine and feminine categories, also known as the dualities. This is not the same as being male or female, or that some signs have more male characteristics and others more female. Instead, within each sign, there is a balance between the two energies, and this is what duality is. This type of balance is present all throughout nature and in other scientific fields, basically what it is saying is that "for every action, there is an equal and opposite reaction." In terms of astrology, this comes in the form of opposing forces, especially opposite signs.

In general, masculine signs are direct and energetic with an outward focus. They prefer using action and are at their strongest when doing so. Sagittarius, Libra, Leo, Gemini, Aries, and Aquarius are the signs with masculine duality.

The feminine signs are more receptive and tolerant of the world around them. They are magnetic personalities, and this shows through with their natural behavior. Capricorn, Scorpio, Virgo, Cancer, Taurus, and Pisces are the signs with feminine duality.

In addition to the dualities, there is also the triplicities, which is when the 12 signs are divided again and put into groups of three based on the four elements: water, fire, earth, and air. Of course, each of these groups also has its own set of characteristics or traits that can be associated with someone of a certain sign.

Earth: These are the practical and stable signs which include: Taurus, Capricorn, and Virgo.

Fire: Fire signs are known as being very active and eager or enthusiastic, these signs include: Aries, Leo, and Sagittarius.

Air: These signs are known for being intellectual and value communication, these signs include: Gemini, Aquarius, and Libra.

Water: These the more emotional and intuitive signs, they include Pisces, Cancer, and Scorpio.

It does not end there. Lastly, we have the quadruplicities in which the signs are divided again but this time into three groups containing four signs. These groups also represent different qualities, and they are divided into cardinal, fixed, and mutable. These are important because these signify how a sign interacts with the world around them.

Fixed: Just like the name sounds, these signs do not like change and are the most resistant to it.

The signs in this group are Leo, Taurus, Scorpio, and Aquarius.

Mutable: These signs are flexible and can adapt easily. People would often describe as the type that would just go with the flow since change does not seem to bother them. The signs in this group are Sagittarius, Gemini, Pisces, and Virgo.

Cardinal: This is the group of signs that are innovative and outgoing. They are often referred to as the initiators. The signs in this group are Libra, Aries, Capricorn, and Cancer.

All of this might seem overwhelming, and when you are first learning about it, it most definitely is. However, once you start to piece everything together, you will see that it fits almost like a puzzle, one that in the end might reveal things about yourself that you didn't know before. That is why this is such a fascinating science; it is personal and quite fun when you learn to use it your advantage. One of the best ways to do this is to use it to find a long-term and compatible partner. This is broken down and best understood in my other book, <u>Astrology: Essential Compatibility Guide to Finding Incredible Relationships and Soulmates</u>. See, what you learn about yourself. This is a unique and fun way to learn about others.

Now that you have all this information, you can put together your very own zodiac profile. It is best to start with yourself, after all, you know you best. You know that the specific location of the celestial bodies plays an important role in your life. You are not an experienced astrologist, but you are more than capable of putting together a simple profile. The rest of the chapters in this book will have more detailed descriptions for you to combine with the information you have already learned about your sign, so you have a more comprehensive profile.

Chapter 4
Aries

March 21 – April 20, The Ram

Those who are born under this sign value and strive for purpose and natural will power. They are often known as fighters, and this shows in almost every aspect of their lives. Aries also have the innate to organize successfully on a grand scale and make great heads of businesses; history has shown us that this sign is also great at helping to organize or develop a country. In general, they resent being criticized by others, but are not afraid of hard work. If you want to reach an Aries with a critique, the way to do so is through logic and reason.

This is an independent sign by choice since they prefer things to be done their way and are not very good at compromising. They will gladly step in and take over if they feel as though someone has lost their sense of purpose. This is one of the reasons they are so successful in the business world because they are not afraid to intervene. However, this also means they are hesitant to let others take the lead and often have too much on their plates because they don't want to give up the responsibility and only trust themselves to do things properly. At the same time, though, this sign is inherently trusting of others which can lead to emotional heartache. They are much wiser in business than they are in their personal lives, but are most compatible with Gemini, Leo, Sagittarius, and Aquarius.

Aries are not usually happy being left at home; their domestic life makes them uneasy or unhappy. For this reason, it is often difficult for them to find a romantic partner that understands them. However, they value and crave affection and sympathy from those around them. Therefore having a healthy romantic relationship is so important for this sign because it can often lead to unhealthy and toxic behavior if their partner is not right for them. You can learn more about the partner that is right for an Aries in <u>Astrology: Essential Compatibility Guide to Finding Incredible Relationships and Soulmates.</u>

This sign has a tendency to be very successful in the workplace and when they set their mind to something, very little holds them back from this. However, this type of success will not bring them happiness, which therein lies the true complexity of this sign. Love and affection are what makes them happiest, but they are difficult to understand at times and are prone to making impulsive decisions.

Aries lack caution and are very quick in action and thought. This is a double-edged sword for them because sometimes it is the right decision and sometimes it isn't. This means that it is easy for them to make enemies and friends, depending on the circumstances. Aries are very ambitious, and it is easy for them to gain both money and position.

They make wonderful friends because they will hold you to the same standards they hold themselves. However, this can be difficult to live up to for some, and there might be some friction from this, but an Aries does appreciate the effort as well. When they decide, they want to learn or accomplish something, nothing will stand in their way. They make wonderful masters, but awful teachers because they are not very good at showing leniency and allowing for mistakes.

All Aries have the same desire of getting a glimpse at the future, mostly because they do not to wait for things to take shape. They would rather jump to the back of the book, then go back and read the middle. Aries like to make predictions about their own futures, but instead of just going with the flow, they will work hard to make sure it comes true if it something they desire.

Aries men, in particular, suffer more in terms of love because they rarely understand the opposite sex and are prone to making many mistakes with them. Aries women are like hurricanes, they often care more about themselves than their partners and can leave emotional destruction in their wake because of this. Aries men and women both take pride in their appearance and expect their partners to as well. This is just another example of the high standards they hold themselves to, which again, they can impose on others.

Aries, in general, are also very happy when they succeed at a goal. This is one of the reasons they are not very good at being home and choose careers where they can climb a ladder. They can feel bored and trapped when they do not have something to work towards.

Chapter 5
Taurus

April 21 – May 21, The Bull

This sign is exactly what you think of when you think of a bull, dominating, strong, and at times stubborn. People who are born under this sign are practical and patient; they approach life with a general sense of caution. This deliberate and careful approach involves everything from their love lives to their finances. However, this sign is not afraid of spending money, far from it actually, they are proud of what they have earned and like to surround themselves with nice things.

One of the most important things to a Taurus is a sense of stability; that is where their cautious approach stems from. They spend their lives searching for true stability and it shows in the decisions they make. They use their endurance, both mental and physical, to their advantage, an important tool that leads to their success. This sign is very good at building and working with their hands, and their careers often reflect this. They do not like to mix their home life with their work life; their job is just that, a way to make money and be financially stable, this is something a Taurus is always aware of. Some of the careers that suit this sign well are farming, banking, building, and teaching.

They are also very good at managing their own finances and make sure to pay their bills on time. Every so often they like to indulge, but overall, they are frugal and prefer to plan for the future rather than make rash decisions in the present.

Domesticity, family, and friends are very important to this sign; they are the first to protect and stand up for the people they love. This behavior can make them come off as domineering or aggressive when really this is just the best way this sign knows how to show love. If you are a Taurus, or you are close to a Taurus, then you know, they are actually quite sensitive and romantic. This sign is not quick to show this side of themselves to just anyone, which can make them across as insensitive or even cold, but this is not the case.

This sign makes a natural host or hostess which shows through with their good taste in things such as food and their innate ability to make a lot out of a little. They also do not easily give into pressure and can remain calm and comfortable when faced with any number of stressors such as overexcitement or fatigue. This can come across as a relentless work ethic, but it comes so effortlessly to this sign that they take it in stride. This is wonderful for them, but they often wonder why others are not capable of doing the same.

This is another sign that takes pride in their appearance, even though they are thought of as Earthy, they too always like to look their best. This means that people often think they are more successful than they are, but they are not quick to judge others based on how they look.

When it comes to personal relationships, Taurus are led by their sensations and passion means less to them than true affection. It was already mentioned that they enjoy the finer things in life and they think affection and romantic relationships are one of these and behave accordingly. This is a sensual sign. They are attentive and loyal to their partners. They are generous and faithful in their romantic relationships and are most compatible with Capricorn, Cancer, Virgo, and Pisces. Just like Aries, they can be naïve when it comes to matters of the heart and can be misled by their own emotions.

One of the faults of a Taurus is that they have a jealous streak that is difficult for them to control. They are incredibly loyal, but their cautious nature makes them wonder if the same can be said for their partners. More often than they care to admit, this can lead to an exhibition of a temper, another fault. They feel sorry for this afterward and is usually not difficult for them to overcome because, in the end, this is a very level-headed sign. They will almost always fall back on their sense of practicality and inner strength.

Those born under this sign have a natural sense of color, harmony, and rhythm that shows through to those around them. They are often successful in the arts because of this but are usually too practical to pursue a career in them. They often choose to keep the arts as a beloved hobby instead, an important part of their home life. This is a strong sign; they make a great friend, and despite their cautious approach, they are fun to be around.

Chapter 6
Gemini

May 22 – June 21, The Twins

This sign is infamous for living up to its name; they are known for having mood swings and having dual personalities. A Gemini would probably describe their brains as constantly pulling themselves in opposite directions, which makes them appear to be both hot and cold, almost in the same moment. Although this can seem confusing, it also means that they are creative thinkers, mostly out of necessity, simply from the way their brains work.

This is a very entertaining and lively sign, but they resist feeling tied down. It is important to understand that a Gemini feels the strain of this natural pull and might even understand it themselves. Their approach to life reflects how their brain operates, to others it can seem disjointed and messy. This is often the case because the Gemini loves with one side of their nature and criticizes with the other, often at the very same time. However, this is natural for them, and they feel most comfortable embracing their nature.

Their innate ability to see all sides makes them great at diplomacy and good problem solvers. Geminis have the gift of dazzling an audience with their wit and sense of humor, which only makes them more magnetic. This sign has no problem attracting a partner but finds it difficult to commit. They also get bored easily, something they strive to prevent from happening. A lot of their energy and time goes into keeping themselves entertained and happy. However, there is an issue with this, because a Gemini doesn't always know what they want out of life. For example, they are ambitious and might work hard to achieve something, but by the time they get it, they are already bored of it and move on to something else. This is so often an issue a Gemini faces, but they will make sure to have fun as they try to figure it all out.

Geminis are wonderful in all forms of communication, and when they do choose a partner, they will only pick someone they think can keep up with them. They can talk about anything for hours and are naturally curious about almost everything around them. Those around them would describe a Gemini as fun and interesting, but often difficult to understand. Their dual personalities mean they are quick to change their minds, and it can be challenging for others to keep up.

If accepted as they are, a Gemini is one of the most delightful and personable signs. It is not until they are being forced to do something that goes against their nature that they show their more negative qualities. Their hearts are constant, faithful, and truthful. The only people who get to see this side of them are those they choose to. This means that the Gemini acquaintances and close friends know are two different people which only adds to their split personality reputation. If you are a Gemini, you have probably experienced this firsthand, that the only people who truly know you, are the ones you deem worthy.

Geminis are known as the life of the party and are inherently good at entertaining. Their devil-may-care attitude might make them seem irresponsible, especially when it comes to finances, but they are actually good at managing their money. Their unique combination of personality traits and natural abilities makes them excel as entrepreneurs if they can stick to something long enough to see it through. They are natural gamblers which can work for or against them depending on the situation.

Geminis are often thought of as walking puzzles, but they love passionately, and when they find the right partner they are devoted and constant. Their friendships are usually long-term, and they are sensitive to other's moods. This makes them wonderful friends, and if you are lucky enough to call a Gemini a best friend, then chances are you will be friends for life. When it comes to romance, they are most compatible with Leo, Aries, Libra, and Aquarius because they are the most likely to accept them as they are.

Appearance is also important to a Gemini, but not in the same way as the two previous signs. Just like with other facets of their lives, they get bored of their appearance and welcome change. They also like to use their appearance as a means of expression, which usually only adds to their appeal.

Chapter 7
Cancer

June 22 – July 22, The Crab

Those born under this sign are thought of as timid, but they are also doggedly ambitious. Their path to success mimics the symbol of the crab, their approach is slow, and when they see what they want, they grasp it and do not let go. This type of technique works well for a Cancer because they are calculating in their decision making, reducing their chances of failure and rejection, the two main things they are afraid of.

Cancers are known as collectors; they are surprisingly good at accumulating things, regardless of if it is good for them or not. This also comes with an unwillingness to throw things away, both of which can come in the form of everything from trinkets to relationships. The opposite of a Gemini in this regard, they are often too constant, and it can be harmful to them because they might stay in toxic relationships or friendships.

This is an ambitious sign, but they usually have a rocky start. However, once they are on the path of success, they will remain that way. The ups and downs of their past motivate them, and part of that usually revolves a need to be financially stable, to make up for this they learn to excel at saving money. This sign values hard work, and with age, they learn to use their sensitivity as a strength, whereas early in their lives it would come across as turbulent emotions.

Cancers are guilty of getting swept up in their emotions they feel at a particular moment. One of their greatest obstacles is learning to control this since it also prevents them from thinking rationally. They might describe their emotions as overwhelming, but as they get older, they will learn to channel this into something more positive through trusting themselves and their intuition.

This sign has an active imagination and makes wonderful musicians, poets, artists, and writers. Their depth of emotion sets them apart from others in this regard, and their success in the arts reflects this. Their overly sensitive nature can also get their own way, making them prone to depression or anxiety. This can happen quickly for a Cancer, for instance, when they feel as though they are not properly recognized. Cancers need to be encouraged and appreciated by those around them, and when they think this is not happening, their own minds can take them a dark place.

Cancers are innately romantic and are especially sensitive to their partner's needs and desires. They are most compatible with Taurus, Virgo, Scorpio, and Pisces because these signs are most likely to provide the recognition a Cancer craves. Despite how their sensitive dispositions can cause them harm, it can also provide them with abilities other, less sensitive signs lack, such as being able to make enlightening predictions about those around them. It is for this reason that they make natural psychics and their intuitions can usually be trusted. Cancers are unusual in that they manage to walk a fine line between being an intuitive and a traditionalist, one of the many reasons they are so interesting.

Cancers can find themselves drawn to the mysterious and are fascinated by other cultures and religions. Cancers have a deep respect for anything that acknowledges and incorporates transformation or progression because they go through so much of it on their own. They relate to change and embrace the idea of coming out of something stronger than they went in. This is one of the main ways they learn to control and embrace their emotions, allowing them to use this as a strength instead of weakness.

It is not recommended that they get married or enter a serious relationship early in their life because they do and will change so much. It is wiser for them to wait, even if others consider them to be late bloomers, going at their own pace will benefit them in the long run. Doing so will increase their chances of finding a partner that will suit them for the rest of their lives, not just who they are during a specific phase of their lives. It is common for this sign to go through many different phases, especially during their more formative years in their teens and twenties, this is true for everyone, but it rings especially true for this sign.

One of the disadvantages of being so sensitive is that Cancers learn how to hide it from people, simply because our world forces them to feel like they must. They often appear more put together and confident than they feel. This façade makes it difficult for them to make friends, but once they do, they make solid, strong friendships. This sign excels at many different careers, but because they are nurturers, careers such as nursing, social work, teaching, or even being a lawyer suit them well because they like setting an example and feeling as though they are helping people.

Chapter 8
Leo

July 23 – August 23, The Lion

Leos are known for being constant and
determined, they value hard work and do not give
up easily. They do not depend on their luck, even
if they would call themselves lucky. Instead, they
place more value and stock in being stable and
secure which is much more important to them.
They resist change for this reason and celebrate
routine and the status quo. Despite having a
strong personality, they can still be perceived as
boring, which is not true. The zodiac teaches you
to take a second look and to not make
assumptions about people, because there is
usually more than meets the eye, and Leos are
certainly proof of this.

This sign is a strong personality who works
tirelessly to rise above the rest; this is part of the
reason they also attract other strong personalities.
This should not be confused as snobbishness
because it is simply not the case, Leos just value
purpose in themselves and others. They will also
forgive almost any fault in those around them if
they feel a sense of common ground. They know
that strong personalities such as themselves are
often alienated for being different and try not to

do that to others, appreciating and celebrating individuality.

Leos make loyal and dedicated friends and are generous with those they care for. This sign trusts easily and appreciates that in others too. This sign is often called the 'heart force of humanity,' because of how sympathetic and generous they are. That being said, it is difficult for them to hold a grudge and they are usually not a very good judge of character since they are so naturally trusting.

They are ruled by the sun, and this shows in the way that they live their lives. Others would describe them as eternal optimists with a connection to the life-giving assets of the sun itself. Leos keep a positive attitude and are a great support system for those around them. Even though Leos are known for having an ego, which they do, their generosity is never compromised.

They are not the best at managing their finances, usually because they haven't had to be, being lucky in money matters. Leos might find themselves getting money from surprising sources, which feels rather normal to them. It is because of this that so many Leos have not had to learn to manage their finances properly. This is something that comes to them with time and experience, though but can cause some problems early on in their lives.

Sadly, even though this sign loves so easily, they are not loved back in the way they seek. They place the most value on love above all else, but because they are so trusting, find themselves in relationships that leave them feeling underwhelmed. They are most compatible with Gemini, Aries, Libra, and Sagittarius because these are the signs that will provide a Leo with the type of love they crave.

Leos are independent and make great leaders because they set such a great example for others. They can inspire and motivate others, often leading people through any number of difficult situations, only to be successful in the end. On the other hand, they make terrible followers and resent being controlled.

This sign is also thought of as a patient and brave. They do not admit defeat easily and show very little fear when facing something that scares them. Leos have a strong constitution and very little shakes them. So, when they seem worried or scared it is for a good reason, they are not one for dramatics or exaggeration. Should a Leo say there is something wrong, it is safe to assume that something is actually wrong.

One of their more positive personality traits is Leo's ability to continue towards a goal regardless of the obstacles that are in front of them. This just goes to show how much they truly value purpose, goals big or small are meant to be achieved, and they tackle everything with the same determination and tenacity. Even while working towards a goal they do not forget about those they care about. At the same time, Leos can also be lazy, and if they feel like something isn't worth it, they will take the easy way out.

Leos might describe themselves as being lonely because they feel isolated and place much worth on the love they feel they don't have. To help make themselves feel better they surround themselves with luxury, but it is not enough to bring them consistent joy since it is not what they really want. If you know a Leo who seems depressed or melancholy, it is usually because they feel like they lack purpose. It cannot be stressed enough; their lives revolve around their function in the world and if they don't think they have one they will feel numb and directionless. This is why Leos thrive so much in positions of power, it reinforces their importance and keeps them on their toes and occupied.

Chapter 9
Virgo

August 24 – September 22, The Virgin

Of all the signs, Virgos are the ones most dedicated to serving others. They are natural caregivers with a deep sense of humanity. Virgos pay attention to detail and are delicate and gentle with others. They have the innate ability to sense what others are in need of and do their best to give it to them. Of course, this is one of the reasons they much such wonderful caregivers

Their approach to life is methodical and analytical, which works well for them because they don't like anything to do unnoticed. This sign is intellectual and generally very successful in life because of it. They choose their friends wisely and are drawn to other intellectual signs. Their judgment makes them successful in matters of business. In addition to their judgment, they are also good at spotting deception and seeking out the truth.

Virgos are often their harshest critics and work very hard in pursuit of their goals. They make great literary critics because they are able to pick out the strengths and weaknesses in equal measure. This sign is one that appreciates and looks for harmony in life. It's easy to see how they do this in their everyday lives, choosing to surround themselves with beauty and elegance at every turn. They like to feel like their surroundings match since it goes into setting their idea of harmony. They even go as far as doing the same for the way they dress; they will gladly spend extra time and energy to look exactly how they want.

Virgos take comfort in rules and laws. They do not resent authority and show respect to those in higher positions or ranks. On the other hand, they do not rest on their laurels and choose to take every opportunity to improve themselves, whether it be intellectually or physically. Virgos enjoy achieving any and all goals they set for themselves and dedicate much of their lives to doing so. They are life-long students and love to learn.

Virgos understand that in order for them to learn things must change and that sometimes they might fail. It is not in their nature to just accept failure, though. Instead, they will learn from their mistakes and emerge stronger and wiser. They are adaptable in the sense that they know they must be, it is part of their rational approach to the world. Virgos think it is impractical to fight against change when it is so essential to life. For that reason alone, they embrace change and accept it for what it is.

Even though they are great caregivers and intellectuals, it is still easy for them to get too wrapped up in themselves. Sometimes Virgos can come off as insensitive or selfish and need to learn to keep themselves in check when this happens. Even when it does, they are not doing it out of malice; they are just simply so detail oriented they can lose sight of the big picture. Of all the signs, Virgos hold the most potential for going to extremes in terms of good and evil. This is just the result of them being too smart for their own good; Virgos have the uncanny ability to justify almost anything if they feel it is for the greater good.

In terms of love, this sign also represents both the best and worst of each of the sexes. If a Virgo chooses a partner that respects and loves them then they will remain warm and inviting to them. Their love lives are not dramatic or overly sentimental but are still not lacking in affection or passion. They do not enter a marriage lightly and consider this type of union as not just a relationship, but a functioning partnership that requires work and dedication to work properly. They are most compatible with Cancer, Taurus, and Capricorn because they too love as intensely as a Virgo.

On the other hand, if a Virgo suffers in their romantic lives, they can become cynical and calloused. Just as a warm relationship will bring out the best in them, a bad relationship will bring out the worst. They do not deal well with disappointment, and a failing romantic relationship is just that, for a Virgo, this can trigger a downward spiral ending with them being overly critical of themselves and others. This will prevent them from pursuing future romantic relationships, causing them to become trapped in a vicious cycle. However, if they use their sound judgment, they can usually stop this from happening by learning from their mistakes. Their practical and often clinical approach to life can save them from themselves, working in their favor.

Virgos are thought of as shy and find it difficult to make friends because they do not typically reach out to others first. If they do, it means they are absolutely comfortable and will make wonderful friends. Virgos are talented observers, and if they do not like what they see, they will hold themselves back on purpose. This is like Gemini who might seem like two different people, Virgos are the same in the sense that their close friends are going to describe them completely differently, then say, a co-worker would since they are not that close with them.

Chapter 10
Libra

September 23 – October 22, The Scales

People born under this sign are very rarely lazy, they are busy bodies and take more comfort in working hard than they do in leisure. They will not choose a partner that does not value hard work because it is so important to them. Libras are very level-headed and do not get angry easily, so when they do it is usually for a good reason.

Libras put a lot of stock in first impressions and have a positive and enthusiastic approach to the world. They combine using their intuition and foresight with practical decision-making skills to when confronted with a problem or an obstacle. They depend on this combination to set them on a path that will lead them to success. This is representative of the balance Libras value so much in their lives. Libras can be both attentive listeners and great conversationalists.

Since Libras appreciate first impressions so much, they like to always look calm and collected, no matter the circumstances. So, even if they are scared, they will try their best to hide their fears from others in favor of a more put together persona. This can work in their favor when it comes to their career because they are masters at appearing calm under pressure, so they make good decision makers. However, it also makes them difficult for others to get to know them.

Financial success is not a priority to Libras, and they will have many ups and downs when it comes to their careers because of this. Libras place more value on peace and justice in their lives than they do money. However, others often seek them out because they are good at mediating arguments and finding common ground that works for all parties involved. As Libras get older, they get more and more talented at incorporating the balance they seek in all aspects of their lives. One of the ways in which they do this is by freely giving and accepting praise.

Libras are at their personal best when they are in partnership with someone because their energies are meant to combine with another's, it is one of the reasons they like balance so much. It also for this reason that they like order and avoid chaos whenever possible. They are most compatible with Gemini, Leo, Sagittarius, and Aquarius because their energies are most in sync with one another. Libras are known to have large circles of friends and are devoted and loyal partners. Even in marriage or long-term relationships, they can't help, but to weigh and try to balance issues too much, which can lead to romantic difficulties.

This sign is considered to be studious in nature and adept at research or study. They will weigh the options from all sides of an issue or subject, giving them the most thorough or comprehensive answer possible. It is because they truly enjoy this type of approach that they will often become a master at a specific topic of study. However, Libras can get so caught up in themselves and problem solving, that they forget about their obligations, making them, at times, unreliable.

Sometimes people call them two-faced, but Libras are just not afraid of change or shifting their mindset if new information presents itself. So, one day they might claim to feel one way, but the next, after finding out new information, will do a complete switch. Keeping up with their constant changing minds can be tiring and confusing. However, this shows a certain amount of resiliency that makes them accept change and continue to move on without getting too caught up in negativity.

Libras have impeccable manners and are known to throw great parties. They have good senses of humor and appreciate wit, finding it very entertaining. Libras are very intuitive and make great psychics and healers if they learn to trust themselves. They will grow more comfortable with themselves as they gain life experience. The end goal of all Libras should be to give themselves a little bit of a break and to learn to see themselves the same way the rest of the world does. They are so caught up with pointing out their flaws that they lose sight of their strengths. Over time this can lead to a very low self-esteem which is very difficult to overcome.

Even though Libras are predisposed to certain personality traits, they are also capable of overcoming that which is harmful to them. They will learn to trust their opinions more and more as time goes on, but until then, they will benefit from relationships in which people point out their gifts instead of their faults.

Chapter 11
Scorpio

October 23 – November 21, The Scorpion

This sign is another that deals with transformation and change, usually revolving around age. When Scorpios are young, they are often religious and virtuous, but when they reach their twenties, they will undergo a dramatic shift. Many of the greatest saints were born under this sign. Even though it is common for a Scorpio's mind to change and for them to seek new experiences and paths, sometimes they dedicate themselves to their faith and feel as though they found their purpose early on.

Scorpios are strong, magnetic personalities who make powerful public speakers. They are not the most logical people, but instead, attract people based on emotions and sentiments. For a Scorpio, this is a strength and not a weakness; they use it to sway the opinions of others easily. Scorpios have a strong sense of curiosity and are thought of as the 'searchers of the zodiac,' because of their insatiable thirst for knowledge. This runs the gamut from spiritual to intellectual pursuits and everything in between, all of which they treat with the same respect and interest.

Scorpios excel in business and politics because of their competitive nature and clever ideas. Instead of being in the public eye, they are better utilized behind the scenes, as advisors or mediators. They are very successful at bringing people together and solving huge issues because they bring more to the table than just logic and reason. On the other hand, they are infamous for procrastinating and will look for any excuse to put something off until a later date. This is not the best habit to have in the business world, so they must learn to adhere to a schedule if they want to be successful. However, once they overcome this obstacle, they are usually very successful in the career they choose.

Scorpios are known to live two different lives, a public and a private life that differ drastically. Scorpios are often too good at this—making it difficult for people to get to know them. In addition, their worst fault is that they are too adaptable to those around them. This combination makes for a person who can come across as both a mystery and fake. Therefore of all the signs, this one has both the most friends and the most enemies. Scorpios are not intentionally hiding anything, they are just doing what comes naturally to them, but it can come across as shady if you don't know them well.

Even if it is not their intention to come off as secretive, they will, just because they are predisposed to it. However, they know there is some power to their ability to live two separate lives, and they can use it to manipulate others into doing things their way. Already a domineering sign, one of the things they need to learn to do is allows others to take the lead. The last thing they need is another manner in which to get their way. However, this is often the case when they figure out exactly how much control they exercise over the image they portray to the public. This is truly both a blessing and curse for the Scorpio, and it is up to their own conscience and willpower to make the right decisions.

Scorpios can become workaholics and can easily push themselves too hard. They are their own toughest critics and despise feeling weak. Instead of allowing themselves this human sensation, they resent it and will just work harder to rid themselves of the feeling. Scorpios constantly seek recognition and more often than not, will also pursue fame on a larger scale, almost as if they have been practicing for it all along. They are good with money and like to surround themselves with luxury, as a matter of fact, they like it so much that a lot of Scorpios will choose to have two sources of income. They are not very good at resting, so having two incomes or careers suits them better than it would other signs that like having down time.

When it comes to matters of the heart, they are passionate and dominating lovers. Sex is a vital part of their lives, but the relationship aspect is mostly a mystery to them, so their partners must be patient and willing to grow and change on their terms. Once they get older, they are usually interested in commitment and will readily direct all of their love and passion towards one person as they will almost always view love as an intense emotion. They are most compatible with Pisces, Cancer, Capricorn, and Virgo because these are the signs that are most willing to let them take the lead.

At some point in their lives, Scorpios almost always develop an interest in occult matters and usually develop intuitive or clairvoyant abilities early in life, giving them, even more, a reason to seek answers. They make wonderful poets, painters, or writers, even if they do not choose to pursue this as a career. They are also known as being eccentric in both appearance and personality, but magnetic nonetheless. History has shown that while Scorpios are capable of fame and fortune, they suffer dramatic ups and downs, often ending in some form of suffering, such as the loss of love.

Part of a Scorpio's journey is likely to include some type of self-destruction, it is one of the things that sets them apart from the other signs. However, so is their ability to learn from it and

54

continue evolving and developing as they should, their resiliency is awe inspiring. It is for this reason that many tragedies are written about this sign.

Chapter 12
Sagittarius

November 22 – December 21, The Hunter

This sign is associated with wisdom and exploring. Sagittarius love to travel and learn as much as they can, they find it enlightening and fun. They are also known to be carefree and independent, but for the right partner, will make love a priority in their busy lives.

They are not known for compromise and have a tendency to see no other way, but their own. This can be challenging for those around them, but with time and effort, they can be swayed. Once they learn to accept new information and methods, it is easier for them to make friends and will do so readily. However, this comes with age, so when they are younger, it is not uncommon for them to have few close friends.

Sagittarius are great workers who devote all their time and energy into whatever goal they are striving for at that specific moment, not stopping until they give into fatigue. They do make great students because they absorb information better on their own from experience, not from a classroom. This does not mean they do not value learning, or seek it out, quite the contrary, they just choose to do so on their own terms.

This is a very curious and open-minded sign, who enjoys learning about other people and attempting to understand them. They make wonderful conversationalists and are energetic and trustworthy. It is also because of these traits that they make such great storytellers and entertainers. Many people born under this sign choose to pursue careers in the arts, especially music and publishing because they naturally excel at these forms of expression.

This sign is prone to restlessness because they have trouble sitting down and relaxing. They get bored easily and prefer instant gratification where they can get it. When a task or goal is taking longer than anticipated to accomplish they might just move onto something else altogether. Even when they are 'relaxing,' they are making plans, and it is for this reason that they are so good in a crisis. No strangers to pressure, because they put enough on themselves, crisis situations tend to bring out the very best in them. They enjoy chaos and get bored of routine, so these types of situations are perfect circumstances that allow them to shine while utilizing the best parts of their personalities.

They are outgoing and personable but are very good at setting healthy limits for themselves, sometimes taking things to the extreme. They will make sudden or rash decisions, often resulting in regrets that their pride prevents them from

57

admitting. This means they are not very good at confessing error and do not like to be proven wrong.

Their greatest fault takes shape when it comes to their personal lives as they tend to marry quickly and regret it later. However, like with most things in their life, they will deny fault and continue to live two lives, putting on the face of happiness, while really feeling discontent. They are most compatible with Leo, Aries, Libra, and Aquarius since they will balance one another out. They are loyal and dedicated in their relationships and if they are happy will strive to keep things from going stale by searching out exciting new things to do as a couple.

People born under this sign enjoy working and feeling as though they are serving a purpose, so going for long periods without employment is not suggested for them because it can cause them negative feelings that are difficult for them to rebound from. Later in life, they tend to seek out a sense of purpose in the form of being avid church goers even if this was not part of their early life.

Overall this is a sign that makes friends for life, especially if they share a love of travel. They are generous with their time and seek out physical and mental stimulation, so they don't get bored. When they feel as though they share these traits with another person, it will only strengthen the bond between the two. Sagittarius do not look for

an abstract connection, but instead are more
likely to make a list of shared characteristics
because that is how they view the world and what
they think is most important.

Chapter 13
Capricorn

December 22 – January 20, The Mountain Goats

Those born under this sign are eyes on the prize types that let nothing stand in the way of them fulfilling their purpose. They take the concept of destiny and work very seriously and put great faith in their own abilities. They are mentally sound and strong, but often not understood by others. They excel at government work or business ventures but do not do very well being at the bottom of the corporate ladder. Capricorns do not like being told what to do and resent what they consider to be the mundane. So, if they feel like it will take years to reach what they think is a respectable position within a company, they might just look for a different job.

Capricorns are one of the only signs that actually get more cheerful as they get older because they finally slow down enough to let themselves enjoy life. When they are younger, they rarely take time from trying to reach their goals for any reason that doesn't suit or propel what they think is their purpose. They are like a dog with a bone when they are younger, not looking up at the world around them. This can cause them to isolate themselves from others; this will only perpetuate their overly serious attitude. Again, as they get older, the more content they are with the goals they have achieved and will allow themselves the chance to enjoy the life the worked so hard for. The foundation they set when they are younger will not go waste, though, as they are hard workers throughout their entire lives, they just learn to find more of work-life balance.

They like to lead because following for them often leads to boredom. They are often seen as being too serious and lacking in humor, which makes others assume they are cold. However, if you get to know them, you will quickly see that beneath the surface they are sympathetic and sensitive people who make great support systems. As you get to know them, you will also see an often dry and subtle sense of humor, one of their more well-known and unique characteristics.

Their ideas about life, love, and duty are not what one would call traditional, which can make it difficult for them to fit in with others. For instance, they put more value on security than most people do which can seem odd for those people who like adventure or value freedom. They do not go out of their way to look for a passionate love affair, their practicality wins out in their love lives as well, another trait that people think is odd.

Even though they are not easily understood by others, they are still great public speakers because they are so meticulous in their planning. This is a good example of how their thorough and almost scientific approach to life pays off in an unexpected way. They are generous with their money, even if they are good at managing it, and routinely donate to charities. They are sensitive to human suffering and generally choose their charities based on this. Capricorns are far from being insensitive or heartless, they are just misjudged.

Fear is at the root of a Capricorn's troubles; this is a life-long battle they fight with themselves. Learning to cope and overcome their fears is something that they must learn to do. However, this does not always come easily and part of it is usually finding the patience and inner calm to allow themselves to begin the long process of chipping away at these fears and frustrations. Everyone has different fears, but for a Capricorn, it generally deals with failure, living without purpose, and feelings of loneliness.

They know they are misunderstood by others because they feel that way, often leading lonely lives. They look for love but are usually unlucky when it comes down to it because they are torn about what they really want. They know that with domesticity comes stability and security, but find themselves fighting against it. This causes a troubled home life, but this is typically only part of their early life. Once they find a suitable partner, they are more likely to embrace domestic life and are less likely to jeopardize the union. They are most compatible with Taurus, Virgo, Pisces, and Scorpio because these signs are also less traditional too.

Capricorns are also artful and delicate, but this is not always seen. They form the best friendships with other Capricorns because they are not as worried about being understood. If you are close to a Capricorn, you know that it usually takes the effort to get to know them, but once you do, you notice what you initially thought is not the whole picture. Many people make the mistake of assuming that people born under this sign are aloof and indifferent, but really they are just unaccustomed to the way in which Capricorns interact with and understand the world around them.

Chapter 14
Aquarius

January 21 – February 19, The Water Bearer

Those born under this sign feel very deeply, but do not show it in the form of physical affection. They also tend to be high-strung and worry too much for their own good, but this is something they can't help. One of their biggest faults is their own ability to cut people down with their words, which they use to hurt people, but usually, come to regret later. If you asked an Aquarian, they would probably admit to having a sharp tongue, but it is not something they are proud of. However, it is also this innate talent that makes them so good at arguing and debating.

Even though they are not very physically affectionate and are terrible at controlling their own worry, they will typically do everything they can to relieve those close to them of their stressors. They can be stubborn in their ideas, but still, value other people's ideas. They are better at making and managing money for others than they are for themselves. They have the uncanny ability to turn anything into a problem they can worry about. This is obviously bad for them but does show that they are creative thinkers with active imaginations.

This sign is rational, open-minded, and love to learn, they are also gifted with the breadth of vision. Their success depends solely on them and their ability to overcome their pension for worry and develop their will-power. If they can do this, there is no position or goal that they can't achieve. Of all the signs, this one has the worst habit and talent for getting in their own way.

Aquarius like to work for a grand cause or purpose because it feeds their idealist nature. They would rather those around them be happy, so much of their life and decisions are based around this idea, and it would suit them if their career could match up with their goals. They are commonly drawn to places where large crowds congregate, and they love the theater and concerts. However, even though they are surrounded by so many people, they would still admit to feeling lonely. This happens to them because even though they have many friends, they will only confide in a precious few. They are not judgmental when it comes to friends and tend to be friends with people from all walks of life.

In general, this not a romantic sign and because of that, they have a negative reputation. It is true that they do not like to be tied down, and not willing to sacrifice their autonomy for a relationship, but if they find someone who respects this, they will be incredibly loyal and devoted. They love deeply, but will never feel fulfilled unless they also maintain a sense of freedom. They are most compatible with Gemini, Libra, Sagittarius, and Aries because these signs are most likely to give them the freedom they crave.

No one would call an Aquarius boring, as they are full of surprises. The water bearer symbol perfectly represents this sign; one vessel is holding water that is alive and the other dead. This symbolizes the separation of good and evil, and the fine line between the two, that Aquarians so often find themselves on. On the one hand, they are smart and creative, but at the same time, these same gifts can be used to hurt those around them.

One of the best personality traits of an Aquarius is their ability to take criticism. They are not fazed by what people say because they do not confuse opinion with fact and this serves them well in their life because they are often criticized. However, they set their own standards for themselves that reflect their own personal values and ideals. A young Aquarius will not be as mentally equipped to deal with critiques like an older Aquarius, who will usually respond with politeness and manners, something that a young Aquarius knows but often chooses to ignore. This is one of their less desirable traits, but they believe everything has a time and place, manners are no exception, making them not necessary all the time. Other signs would adamantly disagree with this because having proper manners is something that they take great pride in. This is just another way in which Aquarius shows their natural talent of choosing good or evil.

This sign isolates themselves and creates such a dependency on technology that they go long periods of time not interacting with people in social situations. In general, Aquarius is unstable, and this translates to moodiness and disorganization. However, no matter how dark they feel, this sign will also represent the light too, which is something the Aquarian should keep in mind since they too have difficulty controlling their emotions. In order for them to be both healthy and happy, they need to find a balance that works for them.

Chapter 15
Pisces

February 20 – March 20, The Fish

People who are born under this sign are known for being kind and gentle. They go through phases and transitions in their lives that show a natural progression unique to their sign. When they are young, they can be impulsive, adventurous, ambitious, and enthusiastic. From a very young age, they possess a natural understanding of the world around them that they did not learn from books or a classroom. They have this because they have the ability to absorb information from experience as well as research. This works in their favor because they like to learn about other cultures and are often fascinated by places they have never been.

They are not very good at managing their finances, which can lead to financial worries. This sign is not very interested in climbing the corporate ladder but will fret over their position in life. One of their greatest fears is being dependent on others, which serves as the main motivator when it comes to their career choice. They are also not very competitive which does not serve them well in today's job market. They might know a subject and feel confident in discussing it, but when it comes to putting it to the test in a more public manner, they will back down without even trying. This devalues their self-worth, something they are guilty of often doing.

When they are younger, they tend to go back on promises because they make a rash decision and agree to something, but when they step back and think about their decision, they have second thoughts. They typically grow out of making these impulsive decisions, but it is something that takes time. This particular personality trait also makes them look flighty and unreliable, but they would describe it as being misunderstood.

Even though the people born under this sign are kind, and would never hurt a friend or loved one on purpose, it is their own worries and insecurities that can cause others harm. This is such a sensitive and thoughtful sign that they are prone to depression and dread asking for help. They view the world as a whole and when things go wrong for them, they assume it is because they are a bad person and no matter what someone says to them, they refuse to believe otherwise. They are also thought to be the most gullible of the signs and will plan their entire week based on a fortune cookie. Again, just like with the impulsive behavior, this is something that they grow out of, they just need time.

This is another sign that enjoys luxury and beautiful things, which does not help them with learning to budget properly. This can pose a real problem when they are younger and still learning to take the time to think their decisions through. Even if they are not sure of their purpose early on, when they find it, they rise to the challenge in a way only a Pisces can. They embrace change to the extent that they make complete, life-changing transformations because of their careers or even their spirituality. These are the people you might not recognize from just a few years previous because so much about them has changed, typically for the better, another one of the perks of experience and age.

They are like Aquarius with their ability to walk the line between two extremes, but in their case, it is crippling shyness and being the life of the party. They are capable of being either, and it comes down their sheer will power that will determine where they fall on the spectrum.

Pisces are extremely intuitive, and this bleeds over into their personal relationships as well, so there is no point in attempting to lie to them. They are romantic and are likely to believe in soul mates more than most. They believe in spiritual bonds and will seek this out in a partner. When they feel as though they have found the one, they are selfless and generous. However, they are not compatible with all signs because they are often too sensitive and emotional. They are most compatible with Cancer, Scorpio, Taurus, and

Capricorn, because these are also emotional signs and they will complement one another in this aspect.

Pisces need to have alone time to help keep them positive and upbeat. Even when they are in a relationship, they will still value their privacy but are not likely to cheat or risk their union. As a Pisces gain life experience, they learn to cope and relate to others in a more natural way.

Additional Books by Author

Astrology: Relationship Compatibility Guide

Other Titles

Empath

Third Eye

Auras

Psychic

Wicca

The link below leads to Valerie's Amazon author page where you can find other Wicca books and much more!

http://amzn.to/2dZA84h

Made in the USA
Middletown, DE
17 February 2017